LANDSCAPE · IN
ITALY

Valley of the Arno from Poppi, Casentino in the province of Arezzo, Tuscany

LANDSCAPE · IN
ITALY

PHOTOGRAPHS BY JOHN FERRO SIMS · COMMENTARY BY LISA ST AUBIN DE TERÁN

PAVILION
MICHAEL JOSEPH

First published in Great Britain in 1989 by
PAVILION BOOKS LIMITED
196 Shaftesbury Avenue, London WC2H 8JL
in association with Michael Joseph Limited
27 Wrights Lane, Kensington, London W8 5TZ

Photographs copyright © John Ferro Sims 1989
Text copyright © Lisa St Aubin de Terán 1989

Designed by Andrew Barron

A CIP catalogue record for this book
is available from the British Library.

ISBN 1-85145-235-4

Typeset in Guardi 55 by The Final Word, Tonbridge, Kent
Printed and bound in West Germany by Mohndruck, Gütersloh
Colour reproduction by CLG, Verona, Italy.

RUINS OF THE GREEK COLONY AT SELINUNTE IN THE PROVINCE OF TRÁPANI, SICILY

SHEPHERD AND FLOCK IN SEPTEMBER, PROVINCE OF SASSARI, SARDINIA

P R E F A C E

ALTHOUGH I have never lived in Italy for any extended period of time, I have a strong affinity with the country; many images of its landscape exercise on me a great emotive pull each time I return. I was born into a rural community in Italy, and lived through all my formative years in another rural community in Shropshire, so it is not surprising that the photographing of the landscape has always been at the heart of my work.

Photographing in Italy, particularly the landscape, has always had a special resonance for me. Since I was a small boy, I have crossed that formidable physical barrier of the Alps many times. Yet even now that journey by train or car and by whichever route, creates an expectancy in me that no short plane flight can ever achieve.

My earliest memories of the journey belong to the days when I travelled by train with my mother and sister. We would set off from Shrewsbury, all clean and excited, and arrive two days later in Milan, dishevelled and exhausted! Later journeys by car were less epic, for my father's Vauxhall Victor had no trouble getting over the Mont Cenis pass. With my own car I have sought to cross by every Western route possible, from a rough track into Liguria at 1700 metres to the fast road through the Mont Blanc tunnel.

Whichever route I take, each journey re-emphasizes the separateness and uniqueness of Italy. All the mountain routes give the impression that the whole of the peninsula is spread out before me. The descent through the tight valleys anticipates the vast plain of the Po and the bright, brilliant south. Never mind the great distances ahead. The flat, sun-drenched road pulls me on, the landscapes of the past mingling with the promise ahead. Sometimes the landscape is familiar, but just as I am different, so too the landscape that I see appears different. It is this continual change, brought about by mood, age, and season, that I, as a photographer, seek to mirror.

Meanwhile I am aware of trying to reconcile two quite distinct attitudes to the landscape. For the Italians typically see themselves

OVERLEAF:
CONVENT CHURCH ON THE
EDGE OF TODI, UMBRIA

within an overall environment and rarely consider the 'landscape' in isolation. Indeed, for centuries the countryside was a dangerous place which rarely evoked pleasurable images. The all too frequent presence of marauding armies, foreign or those of rival neighbours, ensured that. Despite the passage of time, for them the countryside remains, where cultivated, a predominantly working environment, and where not, a place to hunt, gather fungi or other free wild food. There is little room for romantic idealization.

To the outside world, meanwhile, Italy is principally known through its glorious medieval and Renaissance cities. It is this glory that has infiltrated the surrounding countryside and produced a rather disjointed view of the Italian landscape abroad. For instance, the Tuscan landscape – or more precisely, Chianti – represents to non-Italians the quintessential Italian landscape, especially when it includes an isolated farmhouse or castle photographed at the end of a beautiful day in late autumn. The many various shades of russet, brown and ochre are transformed into the very symbols of a past only dimly imagined. 'Chiantishire' has entered our language, and the image bears little relation to the reality of toil in a tough and unforgiving land.

The area south and east of Alba in Piedmont, known as Le Langhe, has many similarities to Chianti but attracts very few tourists. This is probably because there is no Renaissance city near at hand; yet hereabouts many of Italy's best red wines are produced. This is a gentle, undulating and quietly prosperous land of vines, maize and woods, dotted throughout with compact towns and villages, many crowned by medieval castles or fortified houses. On a clear day, the distant, protective, razorback chain of the Alps is easily visible, lending a majestic counterpoint to the harmonious landscape it encloses. I also found open generosity and a lack of pretension, and here, one September morning not long ago, near Barbaresco, I met the brothers Lignana picking grapes. Chatting away, I asked their ages. Here they don't give their ages so much as tell you when they were born. So, the reply was '94 and '96 – of last century, that is. These people don't understand the meaning of retirement.

Last year, I broadened my own knowledge of Tuscany when I discovered the Garfagnana, the valley of the Serchio running north from Lucca, bounded on the west by the Alpi Apuane and on the east by the Apennines. This peaceful, richly cultivated valley has many pleasures to offer, not least the wonderful sweet chestnut woods that proliferate on both sides of the upper Serchio. The unique and strange man-eaten mountains of marble nearby could not provide a more exciting contrast. The quarries, working or disused, have created the most extraordinary shapes.

In Southern Tuscany, I have got to know and love the Maremma, an area stretching south of Grosseto, which from before the time of Dante until after Mussolini finally removed the malarial swamps, was considered to be at the end of the civilized world. Here the landscape changes its coat weekly. At some point of the year, every colour imaginable is present: pale almond and peach in early spring; the vibrant mauve of Judas trees in May; always the soft grey greens of the olive; the full cycle of barley's greens through ochre and soft yellow to the sudden brown of the tilled earth in a short three months; the dazzling luminous yellow of erupting sunflowers which go to seed as you watch; the mysterious colours of the macchia, vaguely green but ever-changing. Other visual sensations come from the tufa (coarse volcanic rock) glowing in the warm colours of sunset or the steam-filled valley near the spa of Saturnia on a frosty winter's morning. Around the ancient towns of Pitigliano, Sorano and Sovana is a landscape embued with the spirit of ancient man's soul.

This year I travelled for the first time the length and breadth of the heel and ankle of Italy, all of which is contained in the province of Puglia. What a revelation it was. Perhaps I was particularly lucky to arrive after an unusually wet spring, for I have never before witnessed such an amazingly abundant profusion of wild flowers. It was not just the quantity of flowers, but their density and even their height! Giant fennel of tree proportions, knapweed, borage, echium, immense fields of waist-high, blood-red poppies and swaying anthemis and, most fantastic of all, large tracts of deep burgundy-flowered clover; a sumptuous carpet guarded by sturdy age-old grey olive sentinels. That part of Puglia, famous for the ancient, extremely picturesque cone-topped stone dwellings known as *trulli*, has a landscape that is unusual for Italy. With its intimate, intricate patchwork fields enclosed by dry-stone walls, hedges and oak trees and intersected by narrow winding lanes, it is reminiscent, to a British eye, of parts of the Welsh Marches or Cornwall.

11

Away from what the Sardinians call 'Il Continente' are the two main islands, both autonomous regions but so different from each other. Sardinia is still a mysterious and wild land despite the inroads made by tourism on the northern coastline. Along the east coast, small towns huddle on ridges or beneath the brooding foothills of the Gennargentu, and where the roads climb and plunge through huge landscapes. This is where one day I followed a newly built, immaculately tarmacked road that zig-zagged crazily up the flank of a mountain whose summit was hidden by low cloud. Suddenly, just as the road began to flatten out, the cloud slipped by and I launched into a blazing, dazzling sun. The air hummed with bees as my nose twitched at the clean fresh scents of this rocky upland. Onwards a few hundred metres the road abruptly stopped. I had a simple choice of three tracks, all unmarked! This too is Sardinia.

For this book I visited Sicily for the first time. Where Sardinia is wild and untamed, Sicily is the opposite. The history of Sicily is the history of European man; every conquering nation for more than two thousand years has left some mark on its land. For centuries Sicily was the granary of the Mediterranean. The island is remarkable today, especially in its centre, for its immense vistas, containing precious few trees and no hedges to define boundaries. Instead you see a quiet, dreamy landscape of undulating contours and subtle gradations of colour: blocks of cream or brown or buff, like some giant rustic carpet drying in the haze of a relentless sun. In contrast, the north and west offer lemon groves and countless acres of vineyards, reminiscent of parts of central Spain.

For me, photographing the landscape is the supremely difficult task of my profession. Even with those special places to which I have often returned and where I have sat, looked, wondered and then photographed, I know there is more to discover. There are always physical relationships to juggle with, textures to assimilate, colours to extract, form to delineate and that mysterious mix of everything which is called the spirit of the place. On the good days I get near to it, on the bad days I see it slip quickly through my lens without leaving even the slightest impression.

John Ferro Sims

13

THE 'PALUDE' IN THE MAREMMA, PROVINCE OF GROSSETO, TUSCANY

IN THE EMILIAN APENNINES SOUTH OF BOLOGNA, EMILIA ROMAGNA

INTRODUCTION

THE phrase 'landscape in Italy' conjures up for me, initially, the places that flit by through a train window. I have lived in Italy, on and off now, for seven years, but it is not so much the places I know well that cling to my memory, as the magic lantern slides of ephemeral views from the thousands of miles of railway tracks that criss-cross the Italian countryside. My train is usually on its way to Milan from either Calais or Paris, and having obliterated France by slicing through it in the hours of darkness, it brings its passengers into the Italian Alps in time for early morning coffee and the first rays of sun. So, after the Italianate herald of the Swiss Alpine towns of Bellinzona and Lugano with its still lake glistening at the feet of the surrounding mountains, Italy begins spilling its villages into the water.

Were it not for the frontier guards at Chiasso and the cursory inspection of the customs officials, however, there would be no way of telling whether the town beyond the platform was in the Italian Canton of Switzerland or in Italy itself. The borderlines have changed too often, and the cultures overlapped through too many centuries for there to be a clear demarcation between one nation and the other. There is a blending effect at Italy's northern perimeter, dominated by Latin shapes and colours.

After the train pulls out of Chiasso, there is a long tunnel cutting its way into Lombardy with an ease that Hannibal would have envied. This is where the Italian lakes begin, stretching away towards the Veneto like a loose tiara of lapis lazuli beads set in the rich filigree of volcanic rocks, draped with woods and studded with towns and villages that have attracted beauty lovers since Roman times. The shores of Lake Garda, in particular, were used, as a playground for Roman Emperors and patricians two thousand years ago. Catullus sang the praises of Sirmium by Desanzano and the garland of mixed woods and other islands that graced its shores. The poet and orator D'Annunzio chose to end his days in a modest villa overlooking Lake Garda above Gardone, with views across its turquoise and blue waters. He converted the house and many hectares of grounds into a monument to himself for the Italian people. It stands to this day, a bizarre homage to both, with every kind and shape of stone and wood worked into its fabric. A First World War battleship has been set into its hill garden reaching out towards the lake that served as a last inspiration to one of Italy's most controversial heros.

D'Annunzio, in this his last architectural gesture, seems to have merely exaggerated what has been a trend across the length and breadth of so many of Italy's twenty-one regions for centuries. Its origins and parameters are hard to define. The natural landscape and the architecture especially of the North are so constantly overlapping that they are interwoven unevenly like a piece of Renaissance brocade. Wherever there are hills, villages cling to them like barnacles to their rocks, huddling around the church and bar. These are villages built of stone quarried four or five hundred years ago. Around each settlement, a fringe of allotments straggles into the surrounding woods.

It was only in 1861 that Garibaldi succeeded in uniting Italy into the country that we know today. Before that, it was comprised of a series of city states and kingdoms. Each state not only had its own character, government and cuisine, it also had its own language. These have survived in modern Italy in numerous forms; they are the dialects that are still a first language to millions, particularly of the older generations. It is not surprising that each of the areas fanning out from the great cities is as proud of its own individual heritage and as fiercely regionalistic as almost any country in Europe. Tuscans and Romans, Genovese and Bolognese and Venetians alike will all tell you that the only truly beautiful place in Italy is where they hail from, and to settle in one area and then move on to another, however briefly, is considered tantamount to treason. The only real agreement to be found north of Rome is in a shared scorn for the South, and the ubiquitous presence of church, bar and allotments. No matter where the patch of earth lies, be it on a swamp, on a ledge halfway up a cliff, beside the railway tracks outside Milan Central station, or tucked down a backstreet in a small town, there are always allotments with a handful of herbs and the statutory tomato plants, aubergine and lettuces, endives and as many vines as can be squeezed into the available space. There is also, usually, mixed in with this soup and salad, at least one ornamental plant: a rose or a cyclamen.

It used to be the Alps that were the great divide, but nowadays an even more impassable obstacle separates the two halves of what is left of the old Roman Empire. It will take more than elephants and ingenuity to break through the barrier of prejudice that exists between the prosperous industrialized North and the arid and still impoverished agricultural South. Mussolini, during his dictatorship, used to send his enemies and suspected enemies into internal exile, forcing them to live in remote southern villages. It was considered to be a form of torture. Carlo Levi, a doctor and painter, was sent to one such village. The land around it looked to him like a wind-beaten sea of chalk; he descibed how from the highest point of the village the eye could sweep across to other identical villages, white and distant on the tops of their hills; punctuating the desolation of Lucania, inland from Taranto. Carlo Levi remembered Lucania as another world, 'hedged in by custom and sorrow, cut off from History and State, eternally patient.' He called it a 'land without comfort or solace, where the peasant lives out his motionless civilization on barren ground in remote poverty, and in the presence of death.' His book is named after a popular saying in the province: *Christ Stopped at Eboli.* The natives claim that they are not Christians because Christ stopped short of their village. By Christian, they mean human; it is a way of saying that the peasants see themselves as mere beasts of burden.

Five decades have passed since the days of the Fascist internments, but fifty years are nothing on the time scale of the South. The conditions of life and many of the customs in rural areas are still as brutally harsh, and the dilapidated houses still cling to the white slopes of clay, overhanging yet more pockmarked clay, barren of trees or grass, where the winds of Africa scorch the earth and only the lizards have an easy life. There are schools, shops and doctors now, but the general air of primitive drudgery and the almost sinister inner tyranny of these villages prevails. The only women to be seen outside their houses are old and draped in dusty black. A few television aerials pierce the skyline, but mostly there are just the patchwork roofs with their thin streams of smoke from the wood stoves that serve for cooking. This is the dark South that fills its

17

Northern neighbours with such dread and spite.

Across the length and breadth of Calabria, in the heel of the boot, and in Puglia and Lucania the earth is scorched in summer; the summers are long, and the land lacks the fertility of more prosperous climes. But although no hope, human or divine, may yet have reached the entrenched poverty there, the beauty of the landscape is often quite startling. I came to know the South in the same manner that I did the North: travelling by train, stopping wherever my fancy took me or hunger struck, or where a particular line came to an end. The train is the most impartial of observers. Its tracks and carriages are impervious to slander, and its presence is so well-known in even the remotest of plains that one can watch the countryside as it passes by without seeming to intrude.

My first sight of Puglia in the early spring was through the windows of a train. I woke up from a restless night of crawling and shunting through the wild, veiled mountains that line the coast of the Abruzzi to find myself confronted with the stunning view of miles of peach and almond trees in flower, holding their pink-flushed blossoms like a gentle fall of snow caught in mid-air. On either side of the tracks, these pointillist fields stretched back to the horizon. From time to time, they would give way to groves of gnarled olive trees with their pale grey, lichen-coloured leaves, and their trunks whose girth was two or three times the size of the olive trees of Liguria on the Mediterranean coast where I once lived. The vineyards characteristic of the rest of Italy had thinned and shrunk to patches of struggling vines. Small flocks of bewildered-looking sheep picked their way between the olive trees, either accompanied by a boy, or else wandering around as though lost.

Also dotted across some of the fields were strange beehive-shaped huts that could have been giant kilns or bread ovens but for the scratched yards around them and the small children scrabbling under washing lines outside their doors. These are the *trulli*, a form of house designed by the Puglian serfs to avoid the strictures of their Norman masters in the middle ages. The peasant was poorer here, perhaps, than anywhere else in Italy, in that he was entirely landless and, to keep him that way, he was not allowed to erect any permanent dwelling on his master's land. A labourer would thus be forced to live in a cave or hovel distant from his place of work. The

Norman estates in Puglia were vast, and a man might have to choose between starving or sleeping out in the open air with the crops he tended. Much of the cultivation was arable, and the peasant would walk to begin his work and then find himself without food or comfort of any kind. The law said that only a temporary hut could be constructed and to comply with the rule, it must be capable of being demolished in a matter of minutes. This was where the *trullo* came into its own. It is a room built of stone without the use of any kind of cement. It is circular and the roof is domed. The removal of the last stone in the roof can pull the entire building down. However, some of the *trulli* still in use today have stood for a thousand years. The stones for building were taken from the rocky soil, and gradually, one *trullo* would be joined on to another by means of a corridor until *trulli* colonies grew up. Traditionally, in anticipation of the birth of a new son or daughter, a new room would be added, and a symbolic masculine or feminine stone would be added after the birth to announce its outcome.

The signs of antiquity are everywhere in Italy, so much so that it can sometimes seem like an enormous museum of past cultures. However, despite its prominence on the tourist maps of Europe, the naturalness with which most Italians not only accept but appreciate their architectural heritage and the beauty of their environment both preserves and enhances them. Roman amphitheatres and temples, Renaissance churches, monasteries and towers are respected, but they are also used. The buildings, the music and the painting are all part of the common domain. The elitism of art in so many other countries does not seem to apply here. This love of music and particularly of opera is something that is found all over Italy.

I lived for a time in a tiny enclosed village built in the Fourteenth Century on a small crag of rock were it sat locked from October to April in a cloud of mist. On a clear summer day one could peer from one of the small shuttered windows across the rolling hills of Siena to the towered town of San Gimignano. On winter days, one could only huddle around the enormous inglenook fire inside the extraordinarily thick and damp stone walls and hope for spring. There was practically no work in the village, for the days of small farmers and artisans had passed with the Second World War, so most of the young people commuted to Siena at the crack of dawn to work in the

19

palatial banks there, or they bussed into Colle Val D'Elsa to work in shops. Otherwise they sat and stared at their fires or out of their tiny windows, depending which season of the year it was. One of the village ladies used to come in and do my ironing, wiling away her time by comparing my cosmopolitan family to her own Tuscan one. She insisted, on several occasions, that she was entirely uneducated, having left school at the age of twelve, and she kept apologizing for this. One day she did this, and then stopped halfway through her sentence to pause and listen to an aria that had just begun on the gramophone. From four bars of the introduction, she picked up the opera and said, 'I love La Bohème, Puccini,' and began to sing the lyrics. After a moment, she remembered what she had been saying and continued to lament her lack of culture.

On my train journeys I meet dozens of fellow travellers from every walk of life, and I often find myself struggling to keep up with their knowledge of Dante, Verdi or Michelangelo. One of the most striking things about Italians is that they have such a genuine love of their land and all the great things that have sprung out of it. However many tourists traipse through their cities and fill their beaches, one always gets the feeling that the natives themselves appreciate them even more, and certainly have a greater understanding of the mysteries of the land and its crops, tied around the skirts of the Catholic Church.

The Catholic religion is an integral part of life here. It seems to be a more benign form of Catholicism than its Spanish counterpart. The centre of every village is its church, but the centre of Italian life is still very much the family. In the cities, the next ruler is fashion, and in country areas it is the land. The rites and festivals of the church are all bound up with these priorities. Much of the Italian day-to-day life is lived on an operatic scale. There is an air of exaggeration and celebration in even the most mundane events. Whatever it is that makes up this characteristic, it does seem to reflect the dramatic beauty of the country that hosts it.

Few places in Europe have more inherent rag-tag colour and gaiety than Naples and its outlying towns. Besides their opera and their ice cream there is a kind of frenzied cauldron of activity, a seething of people and voices. It is life moving at the speed of a cartoon. 'See Naples and die' was said not in reference either to the

ACROSS LAKE COMO TOWARDS VARENNA IN LOMBARDY

grandeur or the squalor of the city, nor even its unassessably high crime rate or its recurrently erupting volcano. Naples used to be a cholera spot. Technology has eradicated the cholera, but nothing can rid the city of its own reigning god. Only San Gennaro, the Roman centurion who was later canonized and whose blood is kept in the city in a glass phial, can protect the Neapolitans – so the popular myth goes. Once a year, the miracle of San Gennaro occurs, when the saint's powdered blood liquefies in the hands of a bishop, in front of thousands of fervent admirers. The chanting, screaming crowd know that if the blood liquefies once more their city will be safe from the ravages of Vesuvius which have devastated their city since its first foundation.

Some years ago, the rites were recognized as pagan and banned by the Pope. The adoration of the phial became so overtly sexual, and the prayers and chants so obscene that the pagan nature of the festival completely took over the Catholic part of the affair, even though the miracle occurred in a church and into the hands of a priest. But Naples refused to forego its miracle, and the Festa di San Gennaro continues apace. Its port, its palaces and its slums are all prey to the caprice of the burning mountain. If it chose to, the volcano could destroy the entire city, spilling boiling lava over its slopes and into the streets themselves. It could turn their world into a desert of grey ash and their dreams to clinker. Only San Gennaro can propitiate the volcano, they say, and if you don't believe it, look at Pompei.

BETWEEN every settlement in Italy and the land that lies around it there is a patchwork of herbs and vegetables, and beyond these, leading away from the village by way of the church, lies the *campo santo*, the cemetery. Napoleon decreed that all the cemeteries must be built away from the villages and outside the town gates, and that is how they remain to this day, white-walled and solitary. Inside, the walls are lined and partitioned like a great macabre chest of drawers, labelled and dated on each rectangular slab of marble to make a chemist's cabinet of death. A miniature black-framed photograph of the deceased often stares out above an epitaph, sometimes with a word of advice or a complaint against the dead relative. The multi-tiered lines of coffins slot into the walls, while the middle space is occupied by the grander tombs of the wealthy, shaded by cypress trees. Some of these tombs are so big that they become chapels, and some of the chapels are so large they are like small houses.

The paths to the *campo santo* will always be well trodden as the graves are kept tended with candles and flowers. Some of the cities have truly enormous cemeteries, laid out like cities in themselves, with streets and avenues flanked by walls of stacked coffins. Genoa in particular has a monstrous cemetery at Staglieno. Generations of stone masons have vied with each other to carve the monuments, vaults and statues that range from angels to anchors. It is a maze of white and grey stone, mostly marble, and like any city it has its suburbs and its centre. The avenue of the illustrious is palatial in its style. One nineteenth-century Genovese street seller was so taken by this pantheon that she determined to reside there, in effigy, herself. She was a nut seller, and she spent her entire life selling nuts and saving her meagre earnings to pay for a statue to be erected at Staglieno after her death. Beside the statesmen and the admirals, poets and generals she stands, nut basket in hand, as a tribute to the city's own respect for its *campo santo* and its sense of democracy.

The crosses and urns, the headstones and touching inscriptions, the lead-lined drawers locked into the graveyard walls and the forlornly gazing photographs can be found everywhere from Trieste to Calabria, but some of the cemeteries tell the history of their inhabitants more clearly than others. Occasionally you see a graveyard which nobody tends: a sure sign of a village forced to emigrate en masse to escape the poverty that could amount to famine at the turn of the century. Following the winding track, you find that the village too is deserted. There are still many ghost villages and hamlets, mostly in Umbria and the South, but occasionally as far north as Liguria, where the stone cottages and hovels sit untouched by anything but rain and cobwebs. The Napoleonic code of laws that is used throughout the country makes it impossible to sell such houses without the consent of all the heirs. Such heirs can run to hundreds with the mounting years and they are scattered like thistledown across three continents. Who can trace, let alone gain the written consent of, the unknown sons and daughters of labourers who emigrated to Australia or America or the Argentine nearly a hundred years ago? It is only in the last twenty years that such rural

23

OVERLEAF:
ACROSS LIPARI TOWARDS
VULCANO, OCTOBER IN THE
AEOLIAN ISLANDS

properties have gained any real value. Sometimes, sons or grandsons return (often speaking no Italian, but retaining a perfect knowledge of their local dialect) to claim such places. More often, though, they remain abandoned as empty tributes to the skill of earlier builders.

Not all the deserted villages are the result of emigration. There are a few more gruesome causes. During the Nazi occupation of Italy reprisals were frequently taken in small rural areas. Of these, Marzoboto is the most famous, and that of Bergiola, in Carrara, possibly the least known. The town of Carrara itself sits at the foot of a marble mountain just inland from the sea in the north of Tuscany. From its mountain, the finest marble in the world is quarried. Michelangelo worked with it, as have sculptors from all over the world. It is the only unveined marble known to man, pure white and flawless. Where the great blocks have been blasted from the mountainside vast white scars stretch down its face and remain visible for miles around.

Bergiola is an ancient settlement perched on a ledge gauged out of the side of the mountain. It has always been a breeding ground of quarrymen. All the men who lived there were deaf to some degree from the noise of their work. The road to Bergiola winds up the mountain through chestnut woods, brambles and broom. On the way, there are several other hamlets, each with its church and cemetery and its own tales to tell. Here, too, the Germans took reprisals, dwindling the population and shrouding the thin, cobbled streets with a cloud that does not lift with the morning mists anymore. High up this road, at the point where it no longer leads on to anywhere else, and where no traffic occurs except for the veering daily bus, Bergiola sits hidden behind its screen of trees. It grew out of the marble trade, and so it is fitting, at least, that its inhabitants now lie under an enormous marble slab. There is just one grey slab for the sixty-four men, women and children who were shot, burnt and battered in a matter of hours in retribution for the murder of a single German soldier who died far away at the foot of the mountain. Most of the men of the village were away, hiding in the hills with the partisans at the time of the massacre, but ironically, had it not been for their quarry deafness, they would have heard the screams of their families. They returned, drawn back by the smoke of the burning schoolhouse where most of the villagers died, in time to bury them, and then to live with the bitter memory.

The quarries still cascade their stones, huge rumbling white lumps that gather at the base and are then hauled away to be cut and graded. The white dust settles everywhere, frosting the trees and rooftops and clouding the river and its streams. Away to the north the ski slopes of the Alps glisten against the skyline, but there are no pistes as impressive as the marble mountain, nor snow as hard.

Not all the migration has been abroad. People say that Tuscany is fast becoming a colony of Sicilians and Englishmen, and, although this is a great exaggeration, there are hundreds of expatriate Britons and thousands of Southern Italians who have settled in the famous blue hills and their valleys. It is too soon to see what lasting mark they will leave on the landscape, but it is hard to believe that the land will remain as unchanged as it has done over the last two thousand years. The Etruscans first tilled and shaped it, steering their ploughs in curves around mounds and trees, and to this day, in a heritage passed from father to son, the old lines are followed. The shapes formed by the bare ochre earth in winter, the young rape and wheat in spring, and the ripe corn in summer, all bend and swerve in the same timeless design, incorporating the hill villages, woods and tracks.

Since Renaissance times Tuscany, unlike the rest of Italy, has been an area of great and small landowners, with the emphasis on the shared ownership of the land. The stone hovels that are to be found elsewhere further north and south do not exist, even for animals, although the prosperity of each family has been subject to the tyranny of climate and war. The *casa colonica,* the stone and brick-built farmhouse with its stabling and stores on the ground and its large beamed rooms above has been handed down and subdivided, cloned and repaired for the last six hundred years. Only since the last war, with its wake of industrialization in Northern Europe, has the population changed. The Tuscans all had a bundle of coins either stitched into their horsehair mattresses, or deposited in their bank accounts, since it was the Siennese, after all, who invented banks and banking. They could afford to build factories, and in so doing they often abandoned their old farmhouses and their land, leaving them to the ravages of wind and rain while they themselves lived in ultra-modern houses built to their own specifications. The

27

English, Germans and Southern Italians merely stepped into their abandoned shoes. As a result of this trend to conserve, early Tuscan architecture, both public and domestic, has remained intact. The churches and the town halls and the private palazzos are as beautiful and awe-inspiring as they were when they were first designed and built by their Florentine and Siennese architects.

Now, the very affluence that made Tuscany great has begun to spoil it. This birthplace of so many great artists and craftsmen – all inspired by the landscape that nurtured them – has preserved its buildings and ravaged its land. Leonardo da Vinci's view of receding hills burning bluer the further away they became is already scarred by cheap and nasty prefabricated factories and warehouses. The hemline of every hilltown is fringed with gaudy concrete blocks. Further north the acne scars of industry are even more apparent, but, somehow, they seem more like an irreverence in Tuscany.

To find some of the loveliest unspoilt spots one must turn, like the farmers with the ancient plough lines, and skirt the old roads to find the oak woods with their rich growth of edible fungi and their herds of wild boar roaming through the maze of their ridged trunks. The wild boar had virtually become extinct in Italy, hounded and slaughtered by huntsmen in such numbers that the native beasts didn't stand a chance. Then, when the chase was over, some of the hunters were so saddened by this curtailment of their sport that they reintroduced the wild boar with a new strain from Hungary. On arrival, these boar showed a very typical romantic attachment to their Tuscan habitat and began to breed. But, instead of their usual litters of one or two young, freak litters of eight and ten were born and thrived on the rich crop of acorns. These have grown into herds that now stampede the cornfields and vineyards and even terrorize lonely farmsteads scavenging in dustbins and rooting through gardens. Consequently, the boar are culled not just by hunters but by worried councils as well. They might well have overrun the entire countryside had it not been for an outbreak of swine fever which has reduced their numbers to a more tenable level. Now they are just one more group of migrants who have settled in the hills.

Whenever I think of Tuscany I think of hills and fields, coloured with the brilliant yellow of rape or the tumultuous scarlet of the poppies, or scored by the contour lines of a plough. The hills may be

PUMICE WASHINGS AND SAND ALONG THE COAST OF LIPARI IN THE AEOLIAN ISLANDS

the gently rolling soothing shapes that catch and pocket sunlight in their dips and folds, or bare craggy outcrops of rock. Towards Siena along the winding backroad from Monteriggioni the previous easy landscape of crumpled velvet that prevails from Florence to Colle Val D'Elsa gives way to an altogether wilder and more dramatic scene. Here the bare rock glints out and sheer cliffs tower above the tops of holm oaks and conifers whose roots have found some tortuous way into its fissures and hidden soil. This is a stronghold of great names. The crags are scarcely divided by smaller claims. The occasional castle or fortress looms out of the stone, but, on the whole, this, like so much of Tuscany, forms part of the great estates.

The poor man may be rich in Tuscany, but the rich man is far richer. Great families like the Piccolouomini, Tolomeo, Visconti and the renowned Medici still own vast tracts of land and superb villas and castles. Back on the more used roads, the ones that fill from nose to tail with foreign number plates in summer, the surrounding contours are more sedate. They seem to reflect the prosperity and the good wines that are culled there from the slopes around Chianti. The vineyards stretch away and swerve into the horizon, patch-worked with startling yellow, gushing red and the infinite variety of green. At times the poppies spread across entire fields swallowing whatever crop was there with their own gaudy hues which narrow, elsewhere, into mere strips lining the roads and ditches.

Christ may have stopped at Eboli and never visited the more remote reaches of Lucania, but he was born in Tuscany and lived and died there. Most of the great Renaissance paintings, the pictorial Bible of the world, were painted there, either on the spot, or else by Tuscan painters who remembered their own homeland and used it as a backdrop to the frescoes and paintings they executed elsewhere. Having grown up seeing so many virgins sitting with their babe in arms under a canopy of the very hills and trees that still stand as they did in the Fourteenth Century, I found the sight of the actual landscape almost unreal. I found that part of the magic of the paintings was the natural magic of Tuscany. The weird light behind so many crucifixions is the strange gathering of colours that occurs just before twilight every night. For years, I was reluctant to stay anywhere in Tuscany for any length of time. I passed through it, weaving backwards and forwards by train, venturing into its cities and towns for just a day or two at a time and then wandering on. The unbelievable prettiness of Tuscany was sacred.

Every year that I spent in Italy, I promised myself that one day I would go and live there: it would be my chosen place; chosen for the beauty of oil on canvas and the generations of poets who had trodden its paths before me. When I finally moved to Casole D'Elsa with the sole purpose of discovering and buying a beautiful house nearby, I realized that the countryside was, in a way, too perfect and the population too changed for me to ever settle there in any permanent way. Tourism and the Twentieth Century account for the latter view, and it is probably a personal insufficiency that must account for the former. I still love to visit Florence and to wander through the wisteria-draped streets of Fiesole with its views across that city. I still love the straddling villas that sit so elegantly on the slopes looking down across the red rooftiles and the Arno. And I still love Lucca; and Siena with its lizard-pillared Duomo and its slanting Campo where the annual Palio takes place. I love the Siennese villas outside the city walls. These are villas built in the characteristic pale bricks of Siena and are light and decorative in style, each one gazing down across its terraces, over palm and cypress trees to a skirt of vineyards, meadows and woods. I love the memory of cornfields in the spring when dusk has settled, bringing with it hosts of fireflies that hover in their hundreds over the fields, lighting up the night in a surreal, suspended carpet of flickering camphor flames.

In fact, when I recall all the beauty of Tuscany, I can scarcely remember why it is that I have turned away from its rolling enchantment. Were Italy not so varied, if it did not have such a feast of alternative beauty to offer, no doubt I would have stayed there. But I am not a hill person: I love mountains. In the absence of these, I love extremes of landscape – dramatic views that stir the less gentle emotions. I would always prefer the Highlands of Scotland to the Home Counties of England. At a daily level, I also admire the spirit of people who have had to battle against their environment as opposed to the more insular contentment of those who have not. For five years before my time in Casole, my view on awakening had been the azure waters of the Mediterranean Sea flanked by the precipitous rocks of Liguria and the hinterland of olive groves and vineyards – and I missed that too.

31

THE Italian Riviera is truly a staggeringly beautiful phenomenon. Staggering because of the sheer height involved, and phenomenon because of the ingenuity and effort that must have gone into making the coastal areas habitable, let alone farmable. When Lord Byron travelled to Milan through the Alps by the Simplon and Lake Maggiore route in 1816, he was astounded by the feats of engineering that had made the Alps passable and wrote in a letter to a friend, 'The Simplon is magnificent in its nature and its art, – both God and man have done wonders, – to say nothing of the Devil, who must certainly have had a hand (or a hoof) in some of the rocks and ravines through and over which the works are carried.' Since Byron's day, these works have been extended to take in almost the entire coastline by both road and rail. Although it was the Romans who built the Via Aurelia, the first great, narrow road from Rome along the coast.

Even without the problems of transport, the sea edge of Liguria runs along a coast that would seem quite unsuitable for human habitation. The rocks rise out of the sea with few places or ledges to build in, and yet, there are hundreds of villages scattered along its shore. Genoa, the birthplace of Christopher Colombus and the capital of Liguria, presides over its wide bay and has always been a major port. Genoa, 'the tightest topographic tangle in the world', climbs up the mountain behind it in a tortuous maze of narrow streets that incorporate both slums and sumptuous palaces. The Barbary pirates plagued this coast for many centuries, and Genoa was a rich prize to sack. When the pirates attacked, boards were placed between one window and its opposite neighbour and the inhabitants escaped across the city. Because of the difficulty of making any flat ground on which to build, once a piece of rock was levelled, the buildings were built as tall as possible, and still tower over the bay.

Despite the great wealth of its capital, Liguria used to be a place riddled with poverty. Those who lived by the sea were fishermen, and those who lived inland farmed sheep and olives. The climate and the land are not propitious for good wine. Notwithstanding the vineyards trickle down the hills, but most of the wine is for home consumption, and is, indeed, of a sour variety. Rather than risk attacking the fortified capital, the Barbary pirates tended to raid the outlying villages along the coast. All the really old ones were built

VENICE FROM THE ISLAND CEMETERY OF SAN MICHELE, VENETO

hidden from the sea, nestled into the seemingly inhospitable folds of the craggy hills, in an attempt to avoid pillage. (However poor these hamlets were, there was always human booty to be taken.) Thus, villages like the twelfth-century Lavaggio Rosso in La Spezia survived: settlements of stone hewn from the surrounding mountain hiding away from prying eyes.

Once the pirates ceased marauding, people began to build their dwellings nearer to the sea, since it was the sea that fed them and provided their meagre living. Some of these are now towns, others are still as small as when they were built in the Fifteenth and Sixteenth Centuries. There is nowhere else left to build there, no conceivable plot of land that a cottage could perch on, no little dip where earth could be carried to and seeds planted. This has been the fortunate lot of the Cinque Terre, five villages carved out of the rock face between Genoa and La Spezia. They were once accessible only be sea, and, although the railway track from Levanto to La Spezia now links them to the outside world, there is still no proper road. Monterosso, Corniglia, Manarolo, Vernazza and Riomaggiore all cluster like limpets on the cliff. Once only fishermen and their priest were to be found there; now it is the fishermen, the priest and a host of daytrippers. These last tramp across the one or two narrow streets of each place and disappear up stepped alleyways with their hiking boots and their knapsacks full of the local Cinque Terre wine, following the course of the Via dell'Amore, the walk that winds along the side of the cliffs in the tradition of the lungomare.

All the villages along this coast have their lungomare, a narrow path cut out of the rock along which one can walk and admire the sea. On clear days the sea glistens in streaks and patches, smoothing its way to and from the horizon. The colour that is most characteristic of this part of the Mediterranean is a rich turquoise interrupted only by strips of green and silvery grey that look like pieces of mirror glass lying under the water. The bands of spume curl onto the sand and rocks in thin trims of pristine lace. Now the small fleets of fishing boats that sometimes line the shores, massing on the business side of the beach, are far out to sea, gathering their multi-coloured catches. When the boats return, morning and evening and in trickles during the day, the reds and greens and blues of the catch all mingle in a phosphorescent glow, in sizes that vary from the tiny anchovies to the sardines and the sword fish. Prettiest of all are the flying fish, combining all the colours of the others in the gossamer of their wings.

On stormy days, when even the old men have been driven off the lungomare by the wind and can no longer sit and gossip or smoke, or fish for squid with their bait of chickens' feet, the sea grows wild. It lashes the coastal villages and pounds along the beaches crashing against rocks and cliffs. It bends the date palms, with their heavy load of old leaves, and twists the wisteria and the oleander trees. On stormy days throughout the winter months the sea turns grey, a greenish grey ridged with thick waves, and the sky turns from its habitual deep blue to a tumultuous blend of colours that quicken and fade from steel grey to pink and even purple. Ruskin, when he visited the Italian Riviera, spoke of the purple rains of Sestri Levante. Although I used to live in Sestri Levante and often saw its purple evening skies, I never saw any purple rain. The finest storms though, the most impressive, are surely the electric storms that rage out at sea, bringing no rain at all, just blindingly bright flashes of light cracking and exploding over the waves like natural fireworks.

Across the precipices and the ravines, and the steep hills and narrow valleys behind them, the mild climate of the coast prevails. It is, of course, cooler inland and uphill where many of the really ornate, balustraded villas sit surrounded by their trellises and terraces looking out to sea. Every building that can, faces out to sea as though to pay homage to the gentle winds and the warm light that lifts from it, and in silent gratitude for the wealth of fish that past generations of fishermen have plundered from its benign and transparent waters. Where there was a poverty of natural materials or the means to buy them, the Ligurians invented them, building great illusionary doorways and windows, or carving fake cornices and statues. Even very simple houses are made grander by the trompe-l'oeil painting on of architectural features. Houses are built of stone and stucco, and the stucco is then richly painted in bright summery colours: yellows and reds and greens and the prevalent rosa ligure.

In winter, the weather changes, but it is always mild – except, that is, in a freak year: in 1983-84 there was snow on the Riviera for the first time in sixty years, and the olive trees that had always grown on the terraces of every available slope since the Ligurians first

35

started planting them there, centuries ago, were killed by the sudden cold and the weight of the snow drifts that sat on them for the weeks of the freak winter. The local people were so excited by the snow when it first arrived that they played with it in the streets, like children, throwing snowballs at each other. Even many of the older people had never seen real snow. Had they known how it was to destroy their livelihood and scar their lands they might not have rejoiced in quite the same way.

Now the silvery grey of the olive groves is blemished, not only in patches, but over entire hillsides, and the rich wild chestnut woods are damaged where the weight of drifts smashed the saplings. With the resilience of a people used to hardship from their land after generations of scrabbling a living from its reluctantly stable topsoil, the locals have replanted the olives, but it will take decades for them to grow back. The hardy vines survived far better, and they still cascade over their stick frames.

Where there is no direct access to the coast, and tourism cannot float the summer economy, the villages are half-deserted. There is no work for the sons and daughters of peasants who once made do with a standard of living that would be totally unacceptable in modern Italy. When I went to live in Velva, a village of farmers skirting a hilltop sanctuary near Castiglione Chiavarese, my baby son was the only young child there, and was cossetted by the dozens of grand-parents who clung to the land they were born on while the world around them changed. Sometimes it seemed that nothing changed up there. The old ladies cooked on their low cast iron, pot-bellied stoves, despite the presence of a brand new gas cooker taking up a great deal of space in their kitchens. These last would be presents from their sons or daughters – accepted but still spurned. Work would begin at dawn on the tortuous terraces and it would end at dusk with enormous bundles of vegetables or firewood being carried home by the bowed and grey-haired workers. At Easter, men from neighbouring villages would carry their crosses from one church to another, tip-toeing with the monstrous weight of the carved cruci-fixes while the entire village would follow behind singing in dirge-like unison. After each rain, when the fungi appeared, everyone would turn out and creep through the woods, gathering the succulent porcini. Just as in springtime troupes of people could be seen

NEAR MATERA, BASILICATA

doubled up, scouring the paths and woods in search of *erbe,* the wild herbs that Italians swear by and eat fresh.

From Sestri Levante with its twin bays, one of white and one of black sand, to Cavi Lavagna with its famous slate quarries and its shingle beach, to Camoglie with its strangely high tenement houses looming over the sea, Liguria sits like the scattered petals of a pretty flower. Lavender, wild thyme and rosemary grow across its slopes together with mimosa and acacia cascading their blossoms until they fall and blow into the sea. In every town the railway tracks cut through the streets before disappearing inside long tunnels and bridging the ravines between them.

During the last war, the presence of these railway tracks and their strategic importance proved to be the downfall of the region. First the British and then the Germans bombed them time and time again, usually missing, and hitting the streets and houses around them. This left great gaps that were filled hastily with apartment blocks and cheap hotels. Some towns, like Zori, were virtually wiped off the map and their replacements are not a pretty sight. The American novelist, Henry James used to wonder why 'the people who but three hundred years ago had the best taste in the world should now have the worst.' In bad taste there is now such a big league that I could not rate the Italians anywhere near the top of it, and yet the modern building is, without a doubt, and almost exclusively, quite hideous. Italy is not alone in having a rash of ugly architecture, but, to quote James again, 'they alone were really to build their civilisation,' and, since they had the foresight and the genius to do it once, I suppose one just somehow expects them to do it again.

WHEN I was a girl I knew Lombardy best, and Reggio Emilia. That was what Italy meant to me: Bologna and Milan, Milan and Bologna, and the railway track between them and approaching them across the Alps from Switzerland. I spent two years there, living alternately for a few weeks in Milan, then for a few weeks in Bologna. Milan always struck me as a grey place to which circumstances kept dragging me back. While there, I lived in a slum tenement by the Naviglio Grande (which, I hear, has since become quite a fashionable part of town). Adolescence, for me, is almost synonymous with staring over the railing into the grey litter-ridden canal watching the bed-springs and the weeds drift along below me like the jetsom of life itself passing me by. The tenement seemed like the hive of a motley swarm of lethargic wintery bees. Out of its tiny windows women hung banners of multi-coloured washing, just as they do in all Italian towns; but our washing, along the Naviglio Grande, was always grey.

In contrast, the times that I spent in Bologna, travelling with my husband of then and his entourage, remain in a haze of warm colours. Bologna is a city of oranges and flames, albeit slightly faded and peeling. Byron called it 'a city celebrated for the production of Popes, Cardinals, painters and sausages'. To me, it was for many years the encapsulation of all that is romantic and beautiful about Italy. I fell in love with the city and the surrounding hills. It was my first love; I used to think of it as a basin of fire, shaped like a great Renaissance amphitheatre.

The slopes around the city have a lightness and a restfulness about them. It is a restfulness peppered with wild flowers, in which I still bask in my memory even though it is nearly twenty years since I was there.

Milan was always more sombre with its flatlands and its rice fields sunk under water, growing the fat arborio rice for all the restaurateurs' risottos. Lombardy is a place of harsh winters and cold winds blowing across its open plains. As the trains pass through its black stretches the tall poplar trees and the willows seem to whisper 'move on.' But Milan is a great centre and it has a magnetic allure and a despotism of its own. To railway riders, it will always be the place to change trains. Mussolini didn't have the preposterously large station built at Milano Centrale for it not to be used. So the city keeps sucking wanderers into its greyness, relieving them at its heart with the wondrous white marble Cathedral and the network of exquisite arcades, before releasing them into the dank fens beyond its long suburbs. The surprise is always the nearness of the lakes. Como, with its dark dripping loveliness is less than an hour away.

On a map, Italy is shaped like a rather fanciful boot which is a very apt symbol for a country that will always have one foot in the sea while the other is firmly planted on the land. Ridging its middle, the Alps and the Apennine mountains descend, with the typical disorder of their settlers, into the sea. On the one side there lies the Adriatic flowing across to Yugoslavia and Greece, on the other, the

39

OVERLEAF:
SUNSET AFTER A STORM,
CASTIGLIONE DELLA PESCAIA
IN THE PROVINCE OF
GROSSETO, TUSCANY

Mediterranean ebbing away to Spain, a country which has often coveted Italy's wealth and power. At the heel of the boot, is the former Kingdom of Sicily, the Jewel of the Mediterranean, an island museum of Europe holding its treasury of Phoenician, Greek and Roman remains. In Palermo, its capital, the palaces abound. Beyond, towering over the volcanic rocks, the temples, theatres and markets at Pegesta and Selinunte are but a sample of the extraordinarily well-preserved testaments of previous cultures. Perhaps the best are at Agrigento, the city that according to legend was founded by Daedalus and Icarus when they flew away from Crete. It is at Agrigento that the Valley of the Temples is found, a Greek city clothed in cypress trees and meadow grass stretched over the uneven escarpments of volcanic rock. Sicily's volcano is Mount Etna, the biggest active volcano in Europe. The mountain and the Mafia, rule the island together.

On the mainland, Vesuvius is the junior volcano, with its own museum of havoc at Pompei. Between the eruptions and the earthquakes, the southern poverty and the droughts, one would think there were enough disasters to make this land accursed. Instead, it seems more blessed than any other I have known, endowed with an indomitable spirit and so great an affection for itself as to make it a pleasure to be in. It is not a very big country, but it is a great country, with a greatness that gorges on its past. It is so varied and, on the whole, so lovely that the best way to see it is not through words but visually. It is hard to describe the quality of light and the quality of life, or the sense of romance and excitement that arrival in a city can bring as the five senses are assaulted all at once. And it is harder yet to convey the still, moody feeling of awe brought on by the tolling of a bell across the countryside from hundreds of different churches at the Angelus when the day ends and the bent backs can straighten and the tired hands rest.

I have not touched on the endless stretches of forest in Umbria, or its capital, Perugia from where the views stretch out further than anywhere else I have been. The eye follows the hills and valleys and the dark lines of conifers across to Lake Trasimene with its weedy pleated shores along which Hannibal's army defeated the Romans, leaving a carnage of dead soldiers to haunt its waters. Perhaps that is where I should have started to describe the landscape, since it is where I have finally chosen to spend half of each year in a huge crumbling villa that my husband and I have bought. Whichever way one looks from the long windows on all four sides of the house there are wild hills and forests, interspersed only rarely by vineyards, and more rarely still by a clinging village.

Nor have I touched on Venice in all her splendour, which is the place where I have chosen to spend the winters of each year, in an apartment overlooking a canal near to St Marks Square. My windows there look out onto water and the palazzo across it, with its gateway and internal garden. On another side, I look into a convent courtyard where nuns sweep the leaves of their oleander trees at six in the morning. The Venetians owed all their prosperity and their safety to the sea and paid their homage to the grey lagoon by building the most beautiful city in Europe on its waters, sinking the marble of Carrara and the oaks of the Veneto into its depths and then constructing an entire city of palaces on top of them, knowing that they had no need of fortification; the treacherous shallows of the lagoon would always protect them from invasion.

On the mainland, and inland, where the corrugated fields can seem, in certain lights, like gilded beaches of rippled sand, the Italians have mirrored another miracle – the feast at Canna. They have turned water into wine. This is a hospitable country where life itself is a feast, and food a sacrament. From the great, gutted, and endlessly rebuilt Rome to the smallest village, life is a daily celebration, an obeisance to ritual, and both a homage and sacrifice to the water and the wine.

Lisa St Aubin de Terán
Venice 1988

SCORCHED OLIVE TREE IN WINTER AGAINST THE VINEYARDS OF CHIANTI, TUSCANY

Vineyards in the southern Gennargentu, province of Nuoro, Sardinia

Olive trees in October, province of Perugia, Umbria

OLIVE TREES IN A FIELD OF CRIMSON-FLOWERED FODDER, A RELATIVE OF CLOVER, IN PUGLIA

SERRAVALLE DI CARDA, SOUTH OF URBINO IN THE MARCHES

NOVEMBER MIST, THE MAREMMA IN THE PROVINCE OF GROSSETO, TUSCANY

VALLEY OF THE TERME DI SATURNIA IN WINTER, PROVINCE OF GROSSETO, TUSCANY

VALLEY OF THE SOLIGNO IN THE PROVINCE OF TREVISO, VENETO

Le Crete in the province of Siena, Tuscany

THE VILLAGE OF STROMBOLI FROM THE SLOPES OF THE VOLCANO IN THE AEOLIAN ISLANDS

54

THE BARE EASTERN SLOPES OF THE ALPI APUANE, TUSCANY

VALLEY OF THE ANAPO AS IT CUTS THROUGH THE PREHISTORIC NECROPOLIS OF
PANTALICA IN THE PROVINCE OF SYRACUSE, SICILY
OVERLEAF: WHEATLANDS OF CENTRAL SICILY

MAIZE GROWING HIGH ABOVE LE LANGHE IN PIEDMONT

SMALL BARLEY FIELDS ON THE FLANKS OF MT TABURNO ABOVE MONTESARCHIO,
PROVINCE OF BENEVENTO, CAMPANIA

NOVEMBER IN THE MAREMMA, SOUTH OF GROSSETO, TUSCANY

61

JUNE IN THE MAREMMA, SOUTH OF GROSSETO, TUSCANY

FIELD FULL OF CORNFLOWERS AND DAISIES, PROVINCE OF LECCE, PUGLIA

ACROSS THE GORGE OF THE GRAVINA TO MATERA, BASILICATA

Near Chioggia in the province of Venice

EEL NETTING 'BOATS', COMACCHIO IN THE PROVINCE OF FERRARA, EMILIA ROMAGNA

FARMHOUSE AND VINEYARDS, PANZANO IN CHIANTI, PROVINCE OF FLORENCE

POPLARS IN THE PROVINCE OF FERRARA, EMILIA ROMAGNA

Forest of the Monastery of Vallombrosa in the Pratomagno, Tuscany

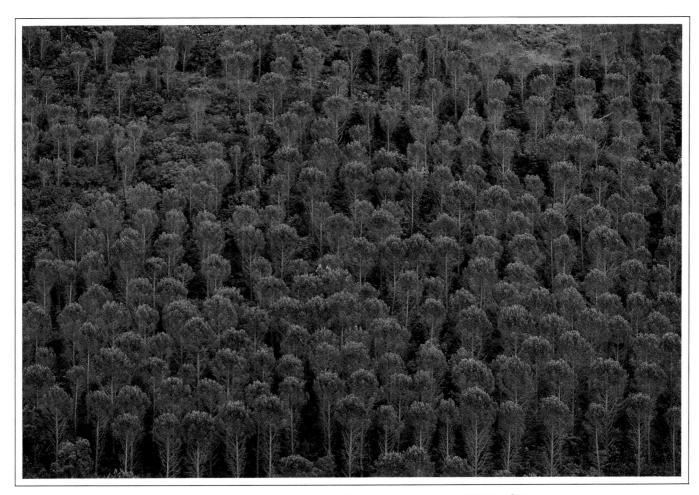

PLANTATION OF UMBRELLA PINES NEAR LANUSEI, PROVINCE OF NUORO, SARDINIA

SUNFLOWERS IN THE MAREMMA, PROVINCE OF GROSSETO, TUSCANY

BOULDERS SCATTERED ON THE WESTERN EDGES OF THE GENNARGENTU, SARDINIA
OVERLEAF: SUNSET OVER THE PLAIN OF FRIULI

74

CASTEL DEL PIANO, MT AMIATA, TUSCANY

GRAVEYARD OF STROMBOLI IN THE AEOLIAN ISLANDS

SWEET CHESTNUT AND HUT IN THE FORESTS OF THE GARFAGNANA,
PROVINCE OF LUCCA, TUSCANY

Sierra d'Orotelli in the province of Sassari, Sardinia

VIEW FROM VOLTERRA TOWARDS THE THERMAL ENERGY ZONE AROUND LARDERELLO IN
THE PROVINCE OF PISA, TUSCANY

WINTER AT THE TERME DI SATURNIA IN THE MAREMMA, PROVINCE OF GROSSETO, TUSCANY

Mountains of the Barbágia Seúlo in the southern Gennargentu,
province of Nuoro, Sardinia

MARBLE-SPOIL CASCADE FROM THE HIGHEST QUARRY IN THE ALPI APUANE, TUSCANY

ROLLING, TREELESS ARABLE LAND IN JUNE, SOUTH OF ENNA IN SICILY

PECULIAR ROCK FORMATIONS NEAR ST TERESA DI GALLURA, PROVINCE OF SASSARI, SARDINIA

OLIVE TREE PRUNED TO ENCOURAGE GROWTH IN THE PROVINCE OF GROSSETO, TUSCANY

CORK OAKS, SARDINIA

THE COAST OF LIPARI AND VULCANO IN THE AEOLIAN ISLANDS

VIEW ACROSS THE FRIULIAN PLAIN TOWARDS THE CARNIC ALPS
OVERLEAF: CRATER OF THE ACTIVE VOLCANO ON STROMBOLI IN THE AEOLIAN ISLANDS

On the banks of the River Merse in the rich iron-ore zone of the Colline
Metallifere, Tuscany

NEAR SÚTRIO IN THE CARNIC ALPS, FRIULI

ROAD LEADING TO RADDA IN CHIANTI, TUSCANY

SHEPHERD AND FLOCK NEAR VOLTERRA IN LATE AUTUMN, PROVINCE OF PISA, TUSCANY

Vineyards above Canelli in the province of Asti, Piedmont

VINEYARDS AND LONE UMBRELLA PINE FROM THE WALLS OF SAN GIMIGNANO,
PROVINCE OF SIENA, TUSCANY

Isola del Giglio from Castiglione della Pescaia in the province of Grosseto, Tuscany

SUNSET AND SIENA, TUSCANY

ROAD FROM SERAVEZZA TO CASTELNUOVO DI GARFAGNANA IN THE ALPI APUANE,
PROVINCE OF LUCCA, TUSCANY

COPPICED MULBERRY TREE IN THE CARNIC ALPS NEAR FRIULI

VIEW ACROSS THE CEDRINO VALLEY IN THE PROVINCE OF NUORO, SARDINIA

THE GENNARGENTU AND TONARA IN THE PROVINCE OF NUORO, SARDINIA

ANDAGNA FROM TRIORA IN THE PROVINCE OF IMPERIA, LIGURIA

BUGGIO IN THE MARITIME ALPS ON THE BORDER WITH FRANCE, LIGURIA
OVERLEAF: TOWARDS ACERENZA, NORTH-EAST OF POTENZA, BASILICATA

BLOSSOMING JUDAS TREES IN MAY, PROVINCE OF GROSSETO, TUSCANY

HAYRICKS IN THE CARNIC ALPS, FRIULI

WILLOW IN A BARLEY FIELD NEAR PIENZA, PROVINCE OF SIENA, TUSCANY

VALLEY OF THE ARNO, CASENTINO IN THE PROVINCE OF AREZZO, TUSCANY

ACROSS THE VALLEY OF THE RIVER FLUMINEDDU, SOUTH OF DORGALI IN THE PROVINCE
OF NUORO, SARDINIA

GUBBIO FROM ABOVE, UMBRIA

SOUTH OF RAVENNA, EMILIA ROMAGNA

Pollard willows in winter, province of Ferrara, Emilia Romagna

'DEFORMED LIPS', A ROCK FORMATION ON THE COAST NEAR ST TERESA DI GALLURA IN
THE PROVINCE OF SASSARI, SARDINIA

A TWENTY-TON BLOCK OF MARBLE AWAITING TRANSPORT IN THE ALPI APUANE, TUSCANY

WOODEN CROSS ABOVE REGGIO IN THE GARFAGNANA, PROVINCE OF LUCCA, TUSCANY

THE PRATO DI SOGLIO (1353m) IN THE CASENTINO, PROVINCE OF AREZZO IN TUSCANY

THE LITTLE ST BERNARD PASS IN JUNE, VAL D'AOSTA

JUNE IN THE DOLOMITES, ABOVE THE ALPI DI SIUSI IN THE PROVINCE OF BOLZANO, TRENTINO
OVERLEAF: THE PLAIN OF LOMBARDY

CANES, PLOUGHED ARABLE LAND AND OLIVE TREES IN THE MAREMMA NEAR GROSSETO, TUSCANY

LONE UMBRELLA PINE IN OCTOBER NEAR VOLTERRA, PROVINCE OF PISA, TUSCANY

The Maremma in May, province of Grosseto, Tuscany

Poplars in the Po delta near Pomposa, Emilia Romagna

PANORAMA BETWEEN CALTABELLOTTA AND SCIACCA IN THE PROVINCE OF AGRIGENTO, SICILY

ARABLE LANDSCAPE IN JUNE NEAR PIAZZA ARMERINA IN THE PROVINCE OF ENNA, SICILY

ACROSS THE VALLE DI BRENTA, CHIOGGIA IN THE PROVINCE OF VENICE

The Tagliamento, Friuli

LANDSCAPE NEAR ASCOLI PICENO, THE MARCHES

ROAD TO PITIGLIANO FROM SORANO IN THE PROVINCE OF GROSSETO, TUSCANY

THE DOLOMITES IN JUNE, TRENTINO, ALTO ADIGE

Near Menaggio, Lake Como

FARMLANDS AROUND VOLTERRA IN THE PROVINCE OF PISA, TUSCANY

CYPRESSES AND UMBRELLA PINES WEST OF VOLTERRA IN THE PROVINCE OF PISA, TUSCANY
OVERLEAF: MOONRISE ON THE PLAIN BETWEEN MATERA IN BASILICATA AND GRAVINA IN PUGLIA

VINEYARDS OF THE COLLIO NEAR CIVIDALE DEL FRIULI IN THE PROVINCE OF UDINE

IN THE HILLS ABOVE ASSISI, PROVINCE OF PERUGIA, UMBRIA

MIXED STRIP AGRICULTURE IN LATE JUNE BELOW CALTABELLOTTA,
PROVINCE OF AGRIGENTO, SICILY

September landscape towards Bitti in the province of Nuoro, Sardinia

Rolling arable landscape in late spring, Volterra in the province of Pisa, Tuscany

LANDSCAPE NEAR FERMO IN THE PROVINCE OF ASCOLI PICENO, THE MARCHES

ACROSS LE LANGHE NEAR CANELLI IN THE PROVINCE OF ASTI, PIEDMONT

TODI IN THE REGION OF UMBRIA

Near Pietragalla in the province of Potenza, Basilicata

THE MACCHIA IN THE MAREMMA, PROVINCE OF GROSSETO, TUSCANY

NEAR URBINO IN THE MARCHES

SPRING VEGETATION IN THE HEEL OF ITALY, PROVINCE OF LECCE, PUGLIA

NEAR SAN DANIELE DEL FRIULI, PROVINCE OF UDINE

SULPHUR FUMAROLES ON THE EXTINCT VOLCANO OF VULCANO, THE AEOLIAN ISLANDS

OVERLEAF: VIEW ACROSS THE COLLINE SENESI FROM THE WALLS OF SIENA, TUSCANY

VINES AND UMBRELLA PINES, ALBERESE IN THE PROVINCE OF GROSSETO TUSCANY

VINES AND UMBRELLA PINES NEAR LECCE IN PUGLIA

THE UPPER VALLEY OF THE ORCIA TOWARDS MONTALCINO, PROVINCE OF SIENA, TUSCANY

HOLM OAKS IN THE MAREMMA, PROVINCE OF GROSSETO, TUSCANY

VALPOLICELLA VINEYARDS IN FEBRUARY, PROVINCE OF VERONA, VENETO

EARLY MAY NEAR MARTINA FRANCA IN THE PROVINCE OF TARANTO, PUGLIA

THE BEACH, STROMBOLI IN THE AEOLIAN ISLANDS